DEADLY CREATURES

DEADLY ANIMALS IN THE WATER

ANITA GANERI

PowerKiDS press

New York

Published in 2022 by The Rosen Publishing Group, Inc.
29 East 21st Street, New York, NY 10010

Originally Published in English by Haynes Publishing under the title: Deadly Creatures Pocket Manual

Cataloging-in-Publication Data
Names: Ganeri, Anita, 1961-.
Title: Deadly animals in the water / Anita Ganeri.
Description: New York : PowerKids Press, 2022. | Series: Deadly creatures
Identifiers: ISBN 9781725331716 (pbk.) | ISBN 9781725331730 (library bound) | ISBN 9781725331723 (6 pack) | ISBN 9781725331747 (ebook)
Subjects: LCSH: Dangerous animals--Juvenile literature. | Dangerous marine animals--Juvenile literature.
Classification: LCC QL100.G35 2022 | DDC 591.6'5--dc23

Design: Richard Parsons

Photo Credits: Cover saulty72/Shutterstock.com; pp. 5, 19 Alamy; p. 6 Ekkapan Poddamrong/Shutterstock.com; p. 7 Getty Images; p. 9 Vladimir Wrangel/shutterstock.com; pp. 11, 13, 25 Oceanwide Images; p. 12 https://commons.wikimedia.org/wiki/File:Great_white_shark_south_africa.jpg; p. 15 https://commons.wikimedia.org/wiki/File:Hippo_closeup.jpg; p. 17 Tory Kallman/Shutterstock.com; p. 21 https://commons.wikimedia.org/wiki/File:Arothron_hispidus_is_kissing_my_camera_at_Big_Island_of_Hawaii.jpg; p. 23 https://commons.wikimedia.org/wiki/File:Gregory_Moine_-_Red_bellied_Piranha_(by).jpg; p. 27 https://commons.wikimedia.org/wiki/File:Stone_Fish_at_AQWA_SMC2006.jpg; p. 29 iStock; p. 30 https://commons.wikimedia.org/wiki/File:Tigershark2.jpg; p. 31 https://commons.wikimedia.org/wiki/File:Scarface-tigershark.jpg.

Manufactured in the United States of America

CPSIA Compliance Information: Batch #CSPK22. For Further Information contact Rosen Publishing, New York, New York at 1-800-237-9932.

CONTENTS

CHIRONEX FLECKERI

BOX JELLYFISH

As its name suggests, the box jellyfish has a box-shaped body, or bell, about the size of a football. It is not only the most venomous jellyfish, but also possibly the deadliest creature in the world. Four groups of tentacles trail from each corner of the bell, each covered in stinging cells.

VITAL STATISTICS

BODY LENGTH:	7.8 inches (20 cm)
WEIGHT:	up to 6.6 lb (3 kg)
EATS:	small fish, prawns
LIFE SPAN:	less than a year
HABITAT:	coasts

DISTRIBUTION:

BOX BEACHES

Box jellyfish live in shallow water off the coasts of northern Australia and Southeast Asia. They are most commonly seen between October and April when they drift close to the shore to breed. Beaches in affected areas put up signs warning swimmers to be careful. Nets are also put in the water, keeping the jellyfish out and the swimmers safe.

DID YOU KNOW?

Box jellyfish are preyed on by sea turtles. For some reason, the turtles are able to eat box jellyfish without being stung.

STINGER FIRST AID

If a person is stung, the wound should be washed with vinegar. This stops the stinging cells from working. Any tentacles should be carefully picked off the skin. Then the victim needs emergency medical help.

The box jellyfish is also known as the SEA WASP or MARINE STINGER.

DEADLY STING

Each of the jellyfish's tentacles measures almost 10 feet (3 m) and is covered in thousands of lethal stinging cells. These shoot tiny darts of venom into any creature that brushes past them. The jellyfish normally uses its venom to catch and kill prey, but it will also sting in self-defense. Box jellyfish hunt alone, during the day. At night, they rest on the seabed.

DID YOU KNOW?

Box jellyfish are strong swimmers. They can shoot along in bursts of up to 6 feet (1.8 m) per second when they are hunting prey.

DEADLY FEATURES

A single box jellyfish has enough venom to kill 60 adult humans. Its sting causes excruciating pain, and death can follow in four minutes, as the fast-acting venom attacks the victim's heart and nervous system.

ELECTROPHORUS ELECTRICUS

ELECTRIC EEL

Found in the rivers of South America, the electric eel lives up to its reputation. It is the world's most powerful electric fish and a top predator. It uses electricity built up in its body to shock and kill its prey of fish and small mammals. In spite of its name, the electric eel is in fact more closely related to catfish than to ordinary freshwater eels.

VITAL STATISTICS

BODY LENGTH:	8 feet (2.4 m)
WEIGHT:	44 lb (20 kg)
EATS:	fish, small mammals
LIFE SPAN:	unknown
HABITAT:	rivers, streams
DISTRIBUTION:	

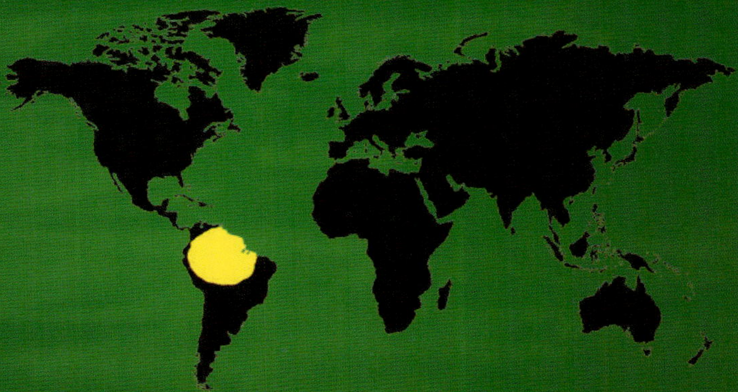

AMAZING EELS

Electric eels have long, snakelike bodies and can grow up to 8 feet (2.4 m) long. Their bodies are covered in thick, slimy skin that helps to protect the eels from their own electricity. A long fin stretches along the underside of their bodies and is used for swimming. The eels live mostly on the muddy river bottom. Unlike most fish, they do not have gills and have to rise to the surface regularly to breathe.

DID YOU KNOW?

Electric eels also use their electricity to find their way around. This is important because they not only have poor eyesight but live in dark, murky water where it is difficult to see.

DEADLY FEATURES

An electric eel has three organs in its body that make electricity. It uses an electric shock to stun its prey, then sucks it into its mouth. An eel can produce a charge of up to 500 volts and, although rare, this would be enough to kill a human.

CARCHARODON CARCHARIAS
GREAT WHITE SHARK

Made famous in the 1970s film *Jaws*, the great white shark is one of the fiercest and most famous hunters in the sea. Its massive, streamlined body is built for speeding after prey, and it has a pointed snout, black eyes, and a crescent-shaped tail.

VITAL STATISTICS

BODY LENGTH:	up to 20 feet (6 m)
WEIGHT:	up to 5,000 lb (2,268 kg)
EATS:	large fish, seals, sea lions, turtles
LIFE SPAN:	about 30 years
HABITAT:	cool, subtropical seas
DISTRIBUTION:	

FIERCE PREDATOR

Great white sharks hunt a wide range of prey, including large fish (such as tuna, rays, and smaller sharks), seals, sea lions, dolphins, and sea turtles. Young sharks eat smaller fish and squid. The shark strikes at its prey from below, taking it by surprise, then catches it in its massive jaws. It then shakes its head from side to side, using its deadly teeth to saw chunks of flesh from its victim's body.

DID YOU KNOW?

Great white sharks have a superb sense of smell for finding their prey. They can smell blood from miles away and can detect a single drop of blood in a million drops of water.

SPY-HOPPING

Great white sharks can lift their bodies and heads out of the water. This is called "spy-hopping" and is also known among whales and dolphins. It allows the shark to look around for prey and other sharks.

SHARK ATTACKS

Great white sharks have a reputation for being ferocious man-eaters. But, in fact, they attack very few people each year. It is thought that these attacks happen when a shark mistakes a surfer or swimmer for its usual prey, such as seals and sea lions. A shark usually attacks at speed with a single bite, then backs away. Most attacks happen at dusk, when sharks are on the prowl for food.

Great whites are also known as WHITE POINTERS, BLUE POINTERS, and WHITE DEATHS.

DEADLY FEATURES

Great white sharks have massive mouths lined with triangular teeth with serrated cutting edges. The lower teeth keep the prey in place while the upper teeth tear off flesh. Like other sharks, great whites have several other rows of teeth, ready to replace any that break off.

DID YOU KNOW?

Great white sharks are very rare because so many have been killed by humans or accidently caught in nets. The sharks are killed for their meat, jaws, and fins, which are made into soup.

HIPPOPOTAMUS AMPHIBIUS

HIPPOPOTAMUS

The hippopotamus lives in and around the rivers and lakes of Africa. This huge plant-eating animal may look like a lumbering giant, but it is one of the most dangerous animals in Africa, claiming far more lives than lions.

VITAL STATISTICS

BODY LENGTH:	up to 16.5 feet (5 m)
WEIGHT:	up tp 4,000 lb (1,814 kg)
EATS:	grasses, sometimes eats dead animals
LIFE SPAN:	30–40 years
HABITAT:	rivers and lakes
DISTRIBUTION:	

GRUMPY GIANT

The hippopotamus spends most of the day sleeping. It keeps out of the hot sun, wallowing in water or mud, and looks for food in the evening and at night. A hippo opens its huge mouth to show its large teeth when it feels threatened. It will charge at any animal that threatens its young or gets between the hippo and the water.

DEADLY FEATURES

Hippos are extremely aggressive creatures and are not afraid of most other animals. Their lethal weapons are their massive bulk and huge teeth. A hippo's lower canines can measure 20 inches (50 cm) and can crush a boat!

DID YOU KNOW?

Hippos sink to the bottom of a riverbed and run along the bottom. Hippos are also fast runners on land and can move at almost 25 miles (40 km) per hour.

ORCINUS ORCA

KILLER WHALE

Killer whales, or orcas, are found in all of the world's oceans, from the Arctic Ocean in the far north to the Southern Ocean in the far south. Famous for their striking black-and-white markings, they live in groups, called pods, of up to 40 animals. The members of a pod stay together for life.

VITAL STATISTICS

BODY LENGTH:	up to 32 feet (9.7 m)
WEIGHT:	up to 6 tons (5.4 mt)
EATS:	fish, seals, squid, whale calves
LIFE SPAN:	50–80 years
HABITAT:	oceans worldwide
DISTRIBUTION:	

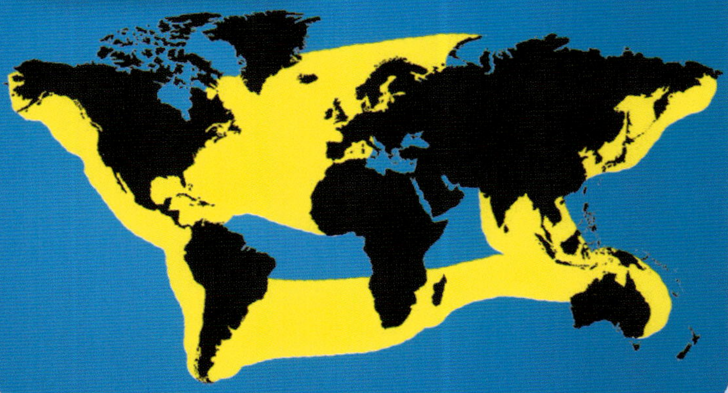

WHALE HUNT

Like wolves, killer whales hunt together in packs. This allows them to catch large animals, such as other whales. The killer whales chase a calf and its mother until their victims are exhausted. Then they separate the calf and stop it from reaching the surface to breathe. Killer whales are opportunistic hunters, but in some areas they may become specialized and mainly hunt one type of prey, depending on the habitat.

DID YOU KNOW?

Killer whales sometimes throw their prey of seals into the air or slap them with their tails to stun and kill them before eating them.

DEADLY FEATURES

Apart from their size and strength, killer whales are also among the fastest animals in the sea. They can swim at speeds of more than 30 miles (48 km) per hour. They have special ways of catching prey.

PHYSALIA PHYSALIS

PORTUGUESE MAN-O'-WAR

The Portuguese man-o'-war looks like a jellyfish. In fact, it is a siphonophore, made up of four different kinds of animal, called polyps. The man-o'-war lives in warm water in the Atlantic, Pacific, and Indian Oceans. It cannot swim, but its sail-like body is blown by the wind or drifts on the ocean currents.

VITAL STATISTICS

BODY LENGTH:	up to 12 inches (30 cm); tentacles 165 feet (50 m)
WEIGHT:	unknown
EATS:	young fish, shrimp
LIFE SPAN:	unknown
HABITAT:	warm seas
DISTRIBUTION:	

SEAFOOD DIET

The Portuguese man-o'-war preys mainly on small fish, young fish, shrimp, and crustaceans, which it traps in its stinging tentacles. The tentacles trail from the man-o'-war's body and can measure up to 165 feet (50 m) long. They "fish" through the water, hoping to catch prey. Then they contract to pull the prey towards the mouth.

DID YOU KNOW?

A tiny fish (*Nomeus gronovii*) lives among the man-o'-war's tentacles and even picks food off them. It is not harmed by the man-o'-war's venom.

DEADLY FEATURES

The man-o'-war's tentacles are covered in venom-filled cells, which are used to sting and kill prey and in self-defense. Tentacles can still sting for hours or even days after a man-o'-war is dead.

TETRAODONTIDAE

PUFFER FISH

With over 120 different species, puffer fish are found all over the world in warm oceans. Most are small- to medium-sized, but some can measure up to 35 inches (90 cm). Although not all puffer fish are poisonous, many are very dangerous. They are thought to be the second-most poisonous vertebrates after poison dart frogs.

VITAL STATISTICS

BODY LENGTH:	up to 35 inches (90 cm)
WEIGHT:	unknown
EATS:	snails, sea urchins
LIFE SPAN:	around 5 years
HABITAT:	coral reefs, mangroves

DISTRIBUTION:

BALLOON FISH

Unlike the porcupine fish, which has long, conspicuous spines that stick out when attacked, a puffer fish's body is covered in tiny spines that are almost like sandpaper. If it is attacked by a predator, it gulps in mouthfuls of water or air and blows itself up like a balloon so that it looks much bigger than it is. Very few animals will try to eat it or even be able to get their mouths around it.

DEADLY FEATURES

Few puffer fish have poisonous spines. It is the skin, liver, and intestines of puffer fish that contain a deadly toxin called tetrodoxin, which is believed to be 1,000 times more powerful than cyanide. If eaten, they can cause paralysis and stop a person from breathing.

DID YOU KNOW?

Puffer fish can blow themselves up to two to three times their normal size. In order to do this, they have very stretchy skin.

PYGOCENTRUS NATTERERI

RED-BELLIED PIRANHA

Piranhas have razor-sharp teeth and a reputation for being ferocious. In the movies, they are shown hunting in shoals, stripping the flesh from their victims' bones in a feeding frenzy. It seems, though, that swimming in shoals is not a form of defense but helps to keep them safe from predators.

VITAL STATISTICS

BODY LENGTH:	up to 13 inches (33 cm)
WEIGHT:	up to 7.7 lb (3.5 kg)
EATS:	fish, insects, crustaceans
LIFE SPAN:	8–12 years
HABITAT:	rivers, streams
DISTRIBUTION:	

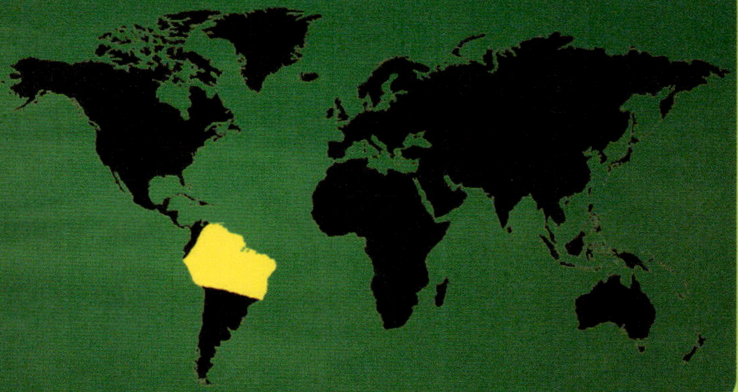

PIRANHA SHOAL

Red-bellied piranhas live in rain forest rivers and streams in South America. They have reddish-brown sides and bellies, and silver-gray backs. During the day, they gather in shoals of 20 to 30 to wait for prey. They mostly hunt fish, snails, and insects. They also scavenge on dead and injured animals. They find their prey by smell or movement, using a set of sensors down the sides of their bodies.

DID YOU KNOW?

Some types of piranhas are vegetarians. They eat seeds and fruit that fall into the river from the bankside trees. Others specialize in eating the fins and scales of other fish.

DEADLY FEATURES

A piranha's sharp, pointed teeth are deadly weapons, used for killing and eating prey. The teeth are tightly packed and lock together. If one tooth breaks off, another grows in its place. Some people use piranha teeth for making tools.

DASYATIS BREVICAUDATA

SHORT-TAIL STINGRAY

Stingrays are fish. They are found in warm, tropical seas, usually close to the shore. Some also live in rivers. The short-tailed stingray lives in the Indian and Pacific Oceans. It has a large, flat, diamond-shaped body, measuring up to 6.5 feet (2 m) across its "wings" and 13 feet (4 m) in length, including its tail.

VITAL STATISTICS

BODY LENGTH:	13 feet (4 m) (including tail)
WEIGHT:	770 lb (350 kg)
EATS:	crabs, shrimp, eels, mollusks
LIFE SPAN:	unknown
HABITAT:	coastal waters
DISTRIBUTION:	

STING IN THE TAIL

The stingray's tail has a long, sharp spike, used in self-defense. Underneath the spike are grooves that make venom. If the stingray is attacked or disturbed, it can suddenly whip its tail around and stick its spike into its victim. Stingrays are usually placid, however, and will only attack if they feel under threat.

DID YOU KNOW?

Stingrays find their food of mollusks, crustaceans, and small fish by smell and using electrical patterns in the water. They stir up the sandy seabed with their wings to uncover their prey.

DEADLY FEATURES

A stingray's spike is needle-sharp and armed with tiny barbs. It can grow more than 15 inches (40 cm) long. It can cause serious injuries in humans and sometimes kill if it pierces a vital organ, such as the heart.

SYNANCEIA VERRUCOSA

STONEFISH

The most venomous fish in the world, the stonefish lives in shallow water along the coasts of the Indian and Pacific Oceans. Its body is mottled brown and gray with flaps of skin and wartlike bumps. Lying on the seabed, it blends in with its background and looks exactly like a weed-covered rock.

VITAL STATISTICS

BODY LENGTH:	up to 14 inches (35 cm)
WEIGHT:	3.3 lb (1.5 kg)
EATS:	fish, shrimp
LIFE SPAN:	5–10 years
HABITAT:	along coasts, coral reefs

DISTRIBUTION:

STONEFISH DEFENSE SYSTEM

Stonefish are preyed on by sharks and rays, and have a lethal form of self-defense. Sticking up from their back is a row of 13 sharp spines. If anything touches the spines, they lock upright and shoot deadly venom into the attacker.

DID YOU KNOW?

Wearing thick-soled shoes can help to protect against a stonefish attack. But it still pays to step very carefully. The spines are strong enough to pierce tough rubber!

DEADLY FEATURES

The stonefish's venomous spines and camouflage are a deadly combination. Swimmers can easily step on a stonefish, mistaking it for a stone. In humans, the venom causes muscle weakness, shock, and terrible pain. Stings are rarely fatal.

GALEOCERDO CUVIER

TIGER SHARK

One of the largest sharks in the world, the tiger shark gets its name from the dark stripes running down the sides of its body. These are easier to see on younger sharks but tend to fade with age. Second only to the great white in its fearsome reputation, tiger sharks have large heads and rounded snouts filled with deadly teeth.

VITAL STATISTICS

BODY LENGTH:	up to 18 feet (5.5 m)
WEIGHT:	up to 1,400 lb (635 kg)
EATS:	fish, seals, seabirds
LIFE SPAN:	45–50 years
HABITAT:	coastal waters in warm seas
DISTRIBUTION:	

SOLITARY HUNTER

Tiger sharks are found all over the world in tropical and warm waters. They usually hunt alone at night. They swim inshore to hunt, returning to deeper waters during the day. Tiger sharks look sluggish but are fast swimmers and reach speeds of over 18 miles (30 km) per hour, but only in short bursts. They have excellent eyesight but rely on their superb sense of smell to find prey.

SACRED SHARKS

Tiger sharks are sacred in Hawaii, where they are believed to be the spirits of ancestors with magical powers. Despite this, thousands of sharks have been killed to make the sea safer for tourists and swimmers.

DID YOU KNOW?

A female shark may give birth to litters of 10 to 80 pups. The pups hatch from eggs inside their mother's body, then are born live.

GARBAGE DIET

Tiger sharks are famous for their huge appetites and their ability to eat almost anything. This has earned them the nickname "garbage sharks." Their prey mainly includes fish, sea turtles, smaller sharks, all kinds of seabirds, seals, and sea lions. They also actively hunt smaller sharks, including other tiger sharks. But more unusual objects, such as lumps of wood, bags of potatoes, car tires, and even a suit of armor have been found inside a tiger shark's stomach. Tiger sharks have also been known to attack people.

DID YOU KNOW?

Apart from stripes, young tiger sharks may also have dark blotches or spots, and are also known as leopard sharks or spotted sharks.

DEADLY FEATURES

Tiger sharks have large, flat, and extremely sharp teeth with finely serrated edges. These teeth are strong enough to bite through bones and turtle shells. They are also curious and aggressive creatures, making them even more dangerous.

GLOSSARY

camouflage to blend in with the surroundings

crustacean an animal with many pairs of legs, a body made up of sections, and a hard shell

habitat the place where an animal naturally lives

mollusk an animal with a soft body, no backbone, and often a shell

paralysis an inability to move parts of the body

prey an animal hunted for food. Also, to hunt another animal for food.

reputation the common opinion about something

serrated having a row of small points, like a saw

venom a poison made in an animal's body

INDEX